Jump and Shout

SCHOOL

CHEERLEADING

TRACY NELSON MAURER

Rourke
Publishing LLC
Vero Beach, Florida 32964

Project Assistance courtesy of Jennifer Tell, Dance and Cheer Factory, Forest Lake, Minnesota.

The author also extends appreciation to Mike Maurer, Kendall and Lois Nelson, the Rourke team, University of Minnesota, and Princeton University. A special thank you to Cheryl Zuber, an extraordinary marching band director.

Photo Credits: Cover, Title, pgs 4, 18, 23, 24, 29, 32, 36, 38, 40, 42, 44 ©PHOTOSPORT.COM
pgs 7, 28 ©Paul Martinez/PHOTOSPORT.COM
pgs 17, 20, 30, 31, 41 ©Peter Schlitt/PHOTOSPORT.COM
pgs 10, 13, 34 ©PIR

Editor: Frank Sloan

Cover and page design: Nicola Stratford

Notice: This book contains information that is true, complete, and accurate to the best of our knowledge. However, the author and Rourke Publishing LLC offer all recommendations and suggestions without any guarantees and disclaim all liability incurred in connection with the use of this information.

Safety first! Activities appearing or described in this publication may be dangerous. Always work with a trained coach and spotters when learning new cheerleading skills.

Library of Congress Cataloging-in-Publication Data

Maurer, Tracy, 1965-
  School cheerleading / Tracy Nelson Maurer.
     p. cm. -- (Jump and shout)
  Summary: "Cheerleaders blend amazing athletic skills and spirited talent to perform breathtaking stunts. They work hard to boost school pride and win over judges at stiff competitions. Coaches expect teamwork, dedication, good grades, and healthy attitudes"--Provided by publisher.
  Includes bibliographical references and index.
  ISBN 1-59515-499-X (hardcover : alk. paper)
  1. Cheerleading--Juvenile literature. I. Title. II. Series: Maurer, Tracy, 1965- Jump and shout.
LB3635.M295 2006
791.6'4--dc22

                    2005012628

Printed in the USA

cg/cg

Rourke Publishing
1-800-394-7055
www.rourkepublishing.com
sales@rourkepublishing.com
Post Office Box 3328, Vero Beach, FL 32964

TABLE OF CONTENTS

Cheerleaders work their magic on and off the field.

Chapter 1

ROUSING GOOD CHEERS

	C'mon, Team!	[Stomp, clap!]
	C'mon, let's fight!	[Stomp, clap! Clap!]
I said,	C'mon, Team!	[Stomp, clap!]
I said,	You're all right!	[Stomp, clap! Clap!]

Cheerleaders yell. They stomp and clap. They jump. They smile from the inside out. Cheerleaders work hard to rouse positive energy from the fans and direct it toward their athletic team. Sound corny? Maybe, but teams say they play harder when they hear the crowds roar.

Supporting the team during the game is just one part of cheerleading today. Cheerleaders decorate the players' school lockers, make and hang team banners, and promote big games around the community, especially homecoming games.

Pep It Up

School cheerleaders plan and perform for pep rallies or all-school **assemblies**. A pep program usually lasts 90 minutes. It features principals, coaches, cheerleaders, the team, the team **mascot**, marching band, and other performance groups. An emcee or a DJ keeps things lively.

Cheerleaders showcase their stunts during pep rallies. They also teach **chants** and play games with the audience, like "TP (toilet paper) the Teacher." Never heard of it? It's a hoot! One student from each grade pairs up with a willing teacher. The first student to cover the teacher from head to toe wins a prize for his or her class—maybe a movie day or pizza party.

Homecoming First

The University of Illinois held the country's first homecoming-week celebration in 1910.

Cheerleading is all about teamwork.

Team athletes should feel like stars at the rally. To add excitement, cheerleaders make break-through banners (tip: cut small vertical slits in the banner to make sure the players burst through). Cheerleaders nail toe-touches, spread eagles, or other jumps and tumbling moves—at least one move as each player's name is called.

Cheerleaders also perform during halftime shows, parades, homecoming celebrations, and community events. They're role models and community representatives. They donate their time and talent to boost walkathons and races for special causes, greet new students at orientation, and teach **cheers** to younger girls and boys. Some school squads compete in cheerleading contests, too.

Cheer for Good Reasons

Schools and communities rely on cheerleaders for their energy, drive, and support. What's the purpose of cheerleading where you live?

- Encourage sports teams.
- Build school and community pride.
- Create a sense of unity and spirit among fans.
- Increase game attendance.
- Rev up school pep rallies, parades, and halftime shows.
- Serve as ambassadors of the school and community.
- Support school and community events.
- Teach cheerleaders teamwork, athletic technique, and leadership skills through supervised training and activities.

School Spirit Everywhere

"Peewee" squads start at the elementary school level. Middle schools, junior high schools, and high schools often sponsor JV (junior varsity) and varsity squads. The varsity squads cheer for the first-string, or A-teams. The JV squads support the younger B-teams. Universities also sponsor cheerleading teams. Many of these squads compete at regional and national contests.

Cheerleaders cheer wherever schools need spirit. You can find cheerleaders across the United States at all types of schools, including schools for the deaf and for the blind. Deafness, blindness, or other challenges like asthma or **artificial** limbs can't stop cheerleaders with true spirit.

True Spirit!

The first deaf squad to qualify for the United Spirit Association's national competition, the California School For The Deaf is just one of many cheerleading groups that beat their physical challenges with super school spirit. The Mason-Dixon Cheerleading Competition brings together deaf cheerleaders from schools in 11 southeastern states. Deaf cheerleaders have earned places on professional squads, too.

Cheerleaders have positive attitudes and strong, flexible bodies.

Chapter 2

ATHLETES AT WORK

Schools usually host tryouts in the spring for the next school year's squad. Coaches look for cheerleaders—male and female—with strong and flexible bodies, willingness to learn, and positive attitudes. Forget movie-star beauty, bodies, and popularity—they're not on the tryout checklist.

Most cheerleading practices involve **aerobic**, or **cardiovascular**, exercises. Aerobic workouts burn calories as they tone muscles. Once you start practicing with the team, your body shapes up while you have fun.

All-season Dedication

School cheerleaders don't follow a set season, like football or basketball players do. Instead, cheerleading requires a long-term commitment. Teams practice for about an hour or more, usually two or three times each week, throughout most of the year.

Cheerleaders also juggle gymnastics and dance classes in their schedules. Coaches like to use tumbling moves, such as cartwheels and handsprings, to put more sizzle into routines. **Choreography** for performances often borrows steps from hip-hop, ballet, jazz, and other dance styles. The extra classes polish the cheerleaders' style.

Beyond practices and cross training, cheerleaders hit the books. Most schools require cheerleaders to carry at least a C or B grade average. Slackers lose their places on the squad.

Learning new words and moves for every cheer works those mental muscles, too. Cheerleaders probably memorize five to ten cheers at first, then add more throughout the school year. They also think up new cheers, organize programs, write and give speeches, and design school spirit boosters. Airhead **stereotype**? Think again.

Cheerleading will take a lot of your time, so make sure you are ready to make the commitment.

Thanks, Parents

What if you make the team? Are you ready for the work? Are your parents?

Parents play a huge part in your cheerleading success. From the start, talk about the commitment you're making. Show them the practice schedule, game schedule, and any other scheduled events. You'll need a doctor's appointment for your physical examination and several signed forms, too.

Your parents might have conflicting commitments and questions about insurance, waivers, and safety. Introduce your parents to the coach and trainers. Offer ideas for dealing with schedule conflicts. Maybe you can car-pool, ride your bike, or take a bus.

Explain to your parents how you plan to manage your time and stay on top of your schoolwork. Go over the team's rules and policies. Most squads expect cheerleading to take **priority** over your other interests. They ask their cheerleaders not to join other sport teams or work a part-time job. Fundraisers cover some of your expenses. Let your parents know the costs. And thank them—a lot.

Chapter 3

HEY, SPORTS FANS

School cheerleaders usually cheer for at least one particular sport team, including football, basketball, soccer, hockey, track, volleyball, wrestling, swimming, or just about any other athletic team.

It helps if you *like* the sport you're cheering. Plan to spend time learning more about it. Study the referee signals. If you can't tell a touchdown from a penalty, you could cheer at the wrong time or for the wrong team. How embarrassing!

Coaches like to see **enthusiasm** for their sports. Invite the athletic team's coach to meet your squad before the season starts. Review the game rules together. Ask when the coaches want you to chant or cheer, and when they do not.

Sports Lettering

Schools in more than half of the United States consider cheerleading a sport. Others call it an activity. It's a complicated debate. Fortunately, most schools agree that cheerleading qualifies for **lettering**.

Typically, a high school or university awards letters for certain sports and activities that require members to demonstrate commitment, skills, and achievement.

Fans know their sport, so make sure you do, too!

Students who earn a letter must meet certain standards. The sport or activity might have a 12-month code of conduct pledge. You promise to follow it 24/7—even when you're not in uniform or in school.

Some coaches, including cheerleading supervisors, test the team on safety, technique, and equipment knowledge. Most teams require attendance at practices, games, and events to qualify for a letter.

Breaking the school rules, ignoring the athletic code of conduct, or sassing the coaches or teachers can spell trouble—as in N-O L-E-T-T-E-R.

Coaches reward qualifying students with a fuzzy, five-inch applique letter to sew onto their letter jackets (often wool jackets in the school colors).

The tradition of earning a letter for participation in a school sport or activity goes back decades.

School Rules

Public schools promise to provide equal opportunity to all students without regard to gender, race, religious creed, color, national origin, or economic status. Cheerleading teams also pledge to reflect the school's values. People watch you more closely than other students, so think before you act!

❈ Display sportsmanship at all times, win or lose. Show courtesy to competitors. Respect officials. Cooperate.

❈ Watch your words. No foul language. No name calling. No rude talk to the teachers, coaches, judges, parents, volunteers, or anyone else for that matter.

❈ Keep your love life private. Swapping spit or sporting a hickey? Gross.

❈ Dress appropriately. Avoid anything too tight, too sheer, or with too little coverage.

❈ Follow all the school rules. No skipping, no cheating. No smoking, no alcohol, no drugs, no steroids. Don't hang out with anybody who dabbles. Don't stay at a party if you see anything off-limits. You could lose your place on the team.

Do you have the spirit?

Chapter 4

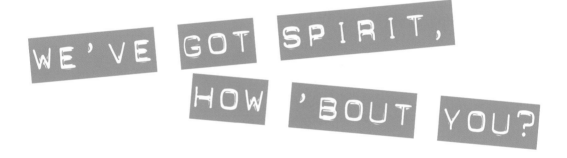

Cheerleaders power up school pride. Their catchy words, songs, and motions energize fans. Cheers and stunts add excitement to the games. Chants—short, repeated phrases—hype the crowds.

Admit it: you couldn't resist joining the cheerleaders when you first heard them chant the classic spirit challenge:

"We've got spirit! / Yes, we do! / We've got spirit! / How 'bout you?"

Cheers and chants raise school spirit. They don't have to make sense, as long as the fans catch on. When Thomas Peebles yelled the first cheer ever in 1884 at a Princeton University football game, he didn't really say anything except the school name:

"Ray, Ray, Ray! / Tiger, Tiger, Tiger! / Sis, Sis, Sis! / Boom, Boom, Boom! Aaaaah! / Princeton, Princeton, Princeton!"

With a few fun words, Mr. Peebles kicked off school cheerleading. Sis! Boom! Bah!

Here We Go, Chanters!

Crowds catch onto chants quickly. They often have a singsong rhythm repeated at least three times and simple claps or hand **gestures**. Also called "sidelines" because you perform them on the sidelines, chants respond to big plays or fill short pauses in the game action.

For **offense** or **defense**, try this classic chant:

Here we go, *Team Name (Spartans, Wildcats, Dragons, Gophers, etc.)*...Here we go! [Clap! Clap!] (repeat)

Good cheerleaders keep the fans involved even when the team is struggling.

When you chant, start with the beat. Clap the rhythm. Then add the words. Start slowly, because the **tempo** speeds up when more people join in. Encourage the crowd between phrases. Yell, "Louder!" Or yell, "Let's go!"

When you're ready to end the chant, add "Last time!" before the final phrase.

Cheerleaders and pep bands work together to keep emotions high.

Musical Chants

Make friends with the school's pep band. These musicians typically perform in the stands, keeping the crowd tuned into your cheers. Learn the school's **rouser** or fight song. Decide on simple moves that fans can do with the song. Cheer them on!

Two easy chants to try with the band:

Charge

The band plays: c-c-c F c F
Then the squad and crowd yell: "Charge!"
The squad yells:… "Again!" or "Louder!" or "Everybody!" or "Last time!"

Tribal Drum Chant

You can do this with just claps, too. A drummer or the band's percussion section taps a slow steady beat, then speeds up, …up, …up!
The squad and crowd clap with the beat, faster and faster.
At the fastest point, the cheerleaders break into jumps, wild pompons, and applause.

Cheers for the Breaks

Save your cheers for time-outs, halftimes, or other longer breaks when the game play has stopped. Longer than a chant, cheers often have several phrases and a distinct ending. Cheers feature stunts and **pyramids**, meaning several stunts linked together.

Need a new cheer? Try this one—then make up verses and your own moves.

Hey you, up in the stands
Get ready to clap your hands
We say [Clap! Clap! Clap! – try a fun rhythm here*]*
And what do you say? [Clap! Clap! Clap! – repeat the same rhythm here*]*
Hey you, all together now
Get ready to yell it loud
Yell it loud (Go Big Red!)
Yell it proud (GO BIG RED!)
Now clap it! [Clap! Clap! Clap! – repeat the same rhythm here*]*
Now yell it! (GO BIG RED!)
Now get it! Let's go!

Creative Combos

Keep a few familiar chants and cheers for every performance. Fans join in faster when they recognize words and actions.

Mix in a few new chants and cheers each time, too. Make note of the crowd reaction—you may find new keepers!

The library and the Internet offer many places to find ideas for cheers. Personalize the cheers with your school colors, team names, and squad style. Experiment with the pacing, rhythm, pauses, and voice pitch. Mix in stomps and claps. Simple is best.

Rhyme Time!

Rhymes help the fans (and you) remember the words. Make a list of team words and words linked to your school name, colors, initials, or mascot. Use a rhyming dictionary for ideas.

COLOR	SAMPLE RHYMES
WHITE	FIGHT, MIGHT, IN SIGHT, TONIGHT, ALL RIGHT
BLUE	YOU, DO, SHOOT TWO, NEW
GRAY	SAY, TODAY'S THE DAY, HEY
GREEN	LEAN, MEAN, FIGHTING MACHINE, BEST WE'VE EVER SEEN
BLACK	WE'RE BACK, ON TRACK, ATTACK
GOLD	SO BOLD, YOU'VE BEEN TOLD, HOT NOT COLD

27

Make Your Moves

Set the cheer's rhythm and add different cheerleading hand, arm, and leg positions. Adapt moves from cheers you already know. Test how the moves flow from one to another. Choreography looks right when it feels right.

Does your cheer call for a stunt? Stunt choreography requires trained spotters and careful planning to make sure everyone stays balanced. Don't risk injury. Ask your coach or trainer for help.

Always practice and perform stunts with a spotter.

Cheerleaders *lead cheers*. You want fans to **interact** with you. "Hit the crowd" after a chant or cheer by making big motions as you move toward the crowd. Jump! Yell, "Cheer with us!" Clap and raise your hands in the air. Keep direct eye contact with one person in the crowd each time.

Wave posters with words from your cheers. Make them ahead of time. Sprinkle the signs with glitter and attach shiny streamers to catch attention.

Chant in the aisles. Play games with the crowd. Toss candy to the loudest section. You'll soon have lots of cheering fans!

Fans take their cue from cheerleaders.

29

Halftime Is Show Time

Your coach helps arrange a halftime show for football games. Generally, halftime lasts about 15 to 20 minutes. That's just long enough to bring a marching band onto the field to play one or two songs. No band? The stadium sound system might be able to handle pre-recorded music.

Treat Them Well

Ordering treats in large quantities at the start of the season saves money. Purchase clickers, pompons, beach balls, T-shirts, or other giveaway items to lob into the stands.

Cheerleaders work with other school groups to make halftime shows exciting.

Cheerleaders create a fun routine that fits the music. Some schools have a mascot, dancers, a pompon squad, a color guard (flag twirlers), or other performance groups. Invite them, too. More performers pack a bigger punch. They also take more time to enter and exit, so keep the show to seven minutes or less.

As the band and performers leave, hit the crowd! Move back into position on the sidelines. Keep jumping and clapping to ride the show's excitement.

Cheer Cheerfully

❁ Stay positive. Cheer for your team, not against the other team. Ignore bratty fans.

❁ Keep smiling. You'll feel better and spread the positive groove around.

❁ Focus on your moves. Make them crisp, accurate, and energetic.

❁ Amp up your voice. Use your diaphragm, not your throat.

❁ Share the workload. Cooperate, accept constructive criticism, and follow instructions.

❁ Enjoy the spotlight and have fun!

Chapter 5

Cheerleading for games takes advance planning. Your coach will probably figure out which cheers, chants, **tumbling runs**, and other crowd-pleasers to practice.

Safety-minded coaches limit cheers and stunts at games to those that everyone has mastered. If you're not ready, the squad looks bad. Worse, someone could get hurt.

One Week Before a Game

❀ Make a checklist of everything the team needs—
megaphones, posters, water jugs, or giveaways. Assign
someone to gather and deliver the items to the stadium.

❀ Hand out a game-day checklist to each cheerleader:
complete and clean uniform, hair ties, pompons, water
bottles, foul or cool weather gear, special shoes or skates.
Note the meeting time and location. Also, bring extra
clothes to change into if you're not going straight
home after the game. Cheerleaders wear their
uniforms only for official appearances.

❀ Agree to the buddy system: nobody goes
anywhere without a buddy.
Cheerleaders in uniform attract attention—
good and bad. Stay aware.

✿ Ask your doctor or pharmacist about side effects before taking prescription or over-the-counter medicines. The drugs can mess with your balance and make you sleepy.

✿ Check the weather forecast for outdoor games. Evening games might turn chilly. Take a sweater or jacket, maybe even gloves and a hat.

✿ Assign one cheerleader to call the cheers and chants. This person watches the game and knows if your team needs a defense cheer or an offense cheer.

✿ Assign a different cheerleader to call the stunts. Perform only the cheers and stunts you've nailed in practices. Make sure you have enough spotters for each stunt.

✿ Assign a spotter to use a hand signal for the flyer, or top performer, during a stunt. Loud crowds make it hard for the flyer to hear. Some spotters tap the flyer's leg along with the count: one tap on the first count, a double tap on the second count and a gentle squeeze on the third "drop" count.

The coach checks that everyone knows the stunt before a performance.

Fans show their spirit.

Just Before a Game

- ❀ Get a good night's sleep. Groggy cheerleaders seldom fire up a crowd.
- ❀ Eat a light snack, not a big meal. You don't want to hurl from a full stomach. You don't want to cheer on an empty stomach, either. Headaches, jitters, and cramps will douse your enthusiasm.

❁ Drink water. Milk is fine, but not before the game. It makes a gurgly croak in your voice. Pack two or three water bottles or sports drinks (not soda, milk, or syrupy-sweet drinks). **Dehydration**, or lack of fluid in your body, sneaks up on you when you're cheering. If you feel thirsty, your body's already too dry. Sip water steadily throughout the game—about a half a glass or 4 ounces (118 ml) at a time.

❁ Double-check your uniform and pompons. Got everything? Is everything clean, polished, pressed, and ready? White shoes should look white, not gray. Take off your jewelry. Spit out your gum. No hair on your face (gals: pull hair back in a ponytail or barrettes; guys: a quick shave).

❁ Arrive 45 minutes before game time. Take 15 minutes to settle your gear and review the game plan. Spend another 15 minutes with warm-up and stretching exercises.

❁ Launch your pre-game cheers 15 minutes before the start of the game. Jump and clap for each team member's name during the introduction—but hold it down during the official announcements.

❁ Honor the flag during the national anthem. Stand with feet together, pompons on the floor. Face the flag and place your right hand over your heart. Wait until the last note of the anthem. Then grab your pompons and cheer, cheer, cheer!

A little pre-game warm-up calms frazzled nerves.

During a Game

🌸 Pay attention. A ball, puck, or even a player might fling out of bounds and into your squad at any time.

🌸 Save your big cheers and stunts for pre-game, halftime, or other major breaks in the action. It's dangerous to perform stunts when the ball or puck is in play. Besides, fans watch the game then, not the cheerleaders.

🌸 Lead cheers, Cheerleader! Dazzling stunts and long routines wow crowds at cheerleading competitions, but they tweak die-hard game fans. Stick to simple chants and crowd activities. Do the wave. Toss goodies. Work with the band.

🌸 Turn sideways to the playing area while you *watch the game*. Don't turn your back to the action, especially if it's close to your area or you could get bonked. Don't turn your back to the crowd, either. And, for Pete's sake, no tugging on your bloomers!

🌸 Ask your coach or volunteer adult to scan the crowd for troublemakers. Keep calm and stay focused if they taunt you or throw stuff down from the stands.

🌸 Follow the team rules. No squirrelly giggles and no sitting with your friends. No boos or other poor sportsmanship.

Football Cheer Factors

When should you cheer or chant? Ask your sport team's coach in advance. Some ideas for football follow here.

- ❊ Before the game
- ❊ During time-outs, but not when a player on either team is hurt
- ❊ Changing offensive/defensive teams
- ❊ Between plays, but not during plays
- ❊ During downtime, but not during official announcements
- ❊ After a decent play, but not after a bad play
- ❊ During halftime

Cheerleaders show their energy and positive attitudes before, during, and after the game.

Pay attention! Sometimes the action gets a little closer than planned.

Knowing when to cheer isn't difficult, but it is very important.

After the Game

❁ Cheer and clap for your team, if they win. Rally for your team if they lose—maybe just applause will do. The athletic team's coach should let you know in advance what the team prefers.

❁ Take ten minutes to stretch your muscles.

❁ Say something nice to the opposing team's cheerleaders, if you haven't had a chance already.

❁ Pick up your mess. Throw away garbage. Leave with everything you brought.

❁ Think about how you'll cheer even better next time!

Remember, your smile is your most important feature.

Further Reading

Cheerleading in Action by John Crossingham.
 Crabtree Publishing Company, New York, New York, 2003.

Let's Go Team: Cheer, Dance, March / Competitive Cheerleading
 by Craig Peters. Mason Crest Publishers, Philadelphia, 2003.

The Ultimate Guide to Cheerleading
 by Leslie Wilson. Three Rivers Press, New York, New York, 2003.

Web Sites

American Association of Cheerleading Coaches and Advisors
http://www.aacca.org/

CheerHome.com, an online information clearinghouse
http://www.CheerHome.com/

Ms. Pineapple's Cheer Page
http://www.mspineapple.com/

National Cheerleaders Association
http://www.nationalspirit.com/

National Council for Spirit Safety & Education
http://www.spiritsafety.com/

National Federation of State High School Associations
http://www.nfhs.org

United Performing Association, Inc.
http://www.upainc.net/

Universal Cheerleaders Association
http://www.varsity.com

Glossary

aerobic (air OH bik) — in exercises, movement that makes the heart and lungs work harder to pump blood and oxygen to the body

artificial (ART uh FISH ul) — made by humans, not "real"

assemblies (uh SEM bleez) — gatherings, meetings

cardiovascular (KARD ee oh VAS kyoo lur) —the heart and blood, especially as they work with the lungs to supply oxygen to the body

chants (CHANTS) — in cheerleading, the short, repeated singsong phrases often performed on the sidelines in response to big game plays or to fill short pauses in the game action

cheers (CHEERZ) — in cheerleading, the longer phrases that usually rhyme and match with gestures and stunts; cheers distinctly start and end, and often occur during time-outs, halftimes or other longer game breaks or at competitions

choreography (KOR ee OG ruh fee) — the plan or patterns for dance steps, movement, or action, usually set to music

defense (DEE fens) — in sports, to stop the other team from scoring or gaining an advantage

dehydration (DEE hy DRAY shun) — loss of water from a body

enthusiasm (en THOO zee AZ um) — excitement or lively interest

gestures (JES churz) — hand or arm movements

interact (IN tuh RAKT) — exchange or communicate with another

lettering (LET ur ing) — in schools, earning a letter or mark of achievement usually for a sport

mascot (MAS KOT) — an animal, person, or thing used by a group as its symbol to bring good luck

megaphones (MEG uh FONZ)— cone-shaped devices that direct sound and make it louder

offense (AH fens) — in sports, to control the ball or puck to gain an advantage or score

priority (pry OR ut ee) — rank or importance

pyramids (PIR uh MIDZ) — in cheerleading, several stunts connected by the top-level, or flyer, cheerleaders

rouser (ROUZ ur) — a fight song or school song

stereotype (STAIR ee oh TYP) — right or wrong, a commonly believed and simple image or idea about a group of people

tempo (TEM PO) — pace or speed

tumbling runs (TUM bling   RUNZ) — two or more tumbling moves, such as cartwheels or handsprings, performed immediately one after the other

Index

About The Author

Tracy Nelson Maurer specializes in nonfiction and business writing. Her most recently published children's books include the *Roaring Rides* series, also from Rourke Publishing LLC. A former drum majorette and color guard member, Tracy lives near Minneapolis, Minnesota with her husband Mike and their two children.